Original title:
The Heart of the Anthurium

Copyright © 2025 Creative Arts Management OÜ
All rights reserved.

Author: Jameson Hartfield
ISBN HARDBACK: 978-1-80581-743-7
ISBN PAPERBACK: 978-1-80581-270-8
ISBN EBOOK: 978-1-80581-743-7

A Dance of Shadows

In a garden so bright, where the sun likes to pout,
Blooms wiggling and giggling, they're dancing about.
Leaves wearing shoes, oh what a sight!
Trying to tango, though none are polite.

Bumbles buzzing, they buzz like they're cool,
While petals are twirling, not following the rule.
One fell on a leaf, a slip not so grand,
It's a jungle ballet, not quite what they planned.

A beetle in shades, he struts with great flair,
As the flowers all laugh, with pollen for hair.
Each bloom tells a joke, with a wink and a grin,
In this botanical party, where fun's sure to spin.

So if you feel low, just take a quick peek,
At the garden of giggles, it's laughter you seek.
Plants sway to a rhythm, so silly and bright,
In the dance of the shadows, everything's light.

Dreams Infused with Color

In a garden wearing fuchsia hues,
The flowers gossip, sharing their views.
What's next on the agenda, they say with glee,
A wild party with petals, just wait and see!

Bees in tuxedos, ready to dance,
They whirl and twirl in a floral romance.
Butterflies giggle, it's quite a sight,
With wings like confetti, they flutter and light!

Echoing Flora

Amidst the green, a chortle escapes,
Where daisies try on funny capes.
Laughing lilacs, in jaunty array,
Whispering jokes, come join the fray!

Tulips tell tales of rainbows and sun,
Chortling together, having such fun.
They sing to the breeze, their voices so bright,
Flora's own choir, a jubilant sight!

Love's Resplendent Layer

Romance blooms under petals so wide,
With mismatched socks, they giggle and hide.
In this garden of laughter, love finds a way,
To sprout little giggles that brighten the day!

Roses wear hats, all quirky and bold,
While the violets trade secrets, stories retold.
Their stems intertwined, a comedic embrace,
In this zany bouquet, love finds its place!

The Rhythm of Nature's Heart

The leaves do a jig, the branches sway,
While raindrops join in, a splashy ballet.
Nature's own drum, a beat so sweet,
Even the ants tap dance on tiny feet!

With a wink and a nod, the sun starts to beam,
Creating bright ripples, like a living dream.
In this amusing waltz, the world spins around,
As laughter and rhythm in harmony sound!

Palette of Nature's Love

In the garden where colors clash,
Petals giggle, creating a splash.
Leaves play hide and seek in the breeze,
Chasing butterflies with the greatest of ease.

Vases filled with pure, vibrant cheer,
Flowers are gossiping, lending an ear.
With each blossom a joke is told,
Nature's laughter never gets old.

Embers of the Tropics

Under the sun, plants dance in delight,
Waving to suitors, what a sight!
Fronds whisper secrets, all around,
Tropical hilarity knows no bound.

Vivid hues have an ego so grand,
Even the waves lend a helping hand.
Swaying in sync, they start a parade,
In this wild fiesta, none are afraid.

Visions in Flora

A rose wore a hat, quite fancy indeed,
While daisies gossip, planting a seed.
Tulips are strutting, what a dandy crew,
Each taking turns to twirl - oh, what a view!

Dance among petals, skip through the grass,
The laughter of blooms tends to amass.
With colors that wink, they jest and they jive,
In this garden, everyone's alive!

Life in Full Bloom

Here's to the blooms with giggles and glee,
Making life brighter for you and for me.
Each blossom a character, playful and bright,
In this verdant circus, day turns into night.

Buds burst with laughter, a joyous release,
Nature's humor is never in cease.
With petals so vibrant, they twirl and frolic,
In this floral world, nothing's symbolic.

Curvature of Life

In a garden of twists and turns,
Plants play hide and seek with the sun,
Leaves dance like they're in a frenzy,
While roots tell tales of having fun.

Buds giggle when they bloom too soon,
Petal parties under the big balloon,
In this jungle where laughter stays,
Life's quirky in so many ways.

Dancing Shadows of Growth

Shadows shimmy when the moon is bright,
Plants waltz in the soft twilight,
Laughter echoes in the cool night air,
As blossoms spin without a care.

A stem that trips, a leaf that falls,
They giggle and bounce off garden walls,
Rooted in joy, they sway and sway,
Making the most of the bright bouquet.

Enveloped in Petals

Petals cozy in their fanciful wraps,
Budding jokes in their snug little naps,
They whisper secrets to the buzzing bees,
And share punchlines with the wandering breeze.

Dressed in hues that make them smile,
Puns bloom freely, in carefree style,
Each flower grins in its own way,
Spreading cheer all through the day.

Celestial Flora

Stars twinkle in the garden's crown,
While blossoms prance with a vibrant frown,
Wishing on wishes that flutter by,
Planting their dreams in the starry sky.

They laugh at clouds in a playful chase,
Sprinkling joy in this silly place,
Twisting, turning in a merry loop,
Creating a cosmic, floral troop.

Dance of the Tropics

In the jungle, plants do groove,
With petals swaying to the move.
Laughter bounces in the air,
As ferns and flowers dance with flair.

Coconuts join in the fun,
Hula hoops spun by the sun.
Leaves do cha-cha, what a sight,
Even the insects feel the bite!

Tropical tunes draw all around,
Frogs leap high, making a sound.
The mangoes twist, the papayas cheer,
In this wild party, all's quite clear!

So when you're down, just take a chance,
Join the plants in their tropical dance.
You'll find your worries float away,
As blossoms bloom and sway all day.

Petal Fire

Bright colors burst, a floral blaze,
Like fireworks in summer's haze.
Each bloom winks, a cheeky tease,
With petals that sway in the breeze.

A rose laughs in a vibrant hat,
While daisies gossip about the cat.
Frangipanis play hide and seek,
In this garden, they're all unique!

Some flowers strut like they own the show,
While others twirl, saying, "Look at me go!"
It's a riot of whimsies in the sun,
Where petals are playful and so much fun!

So if you stumble on this delight,
Join the flowers for a silly night.
With each petal's laugh, joy will inspire,
In this garden of lively petal fire.

Secrets of a Flourishing Bloom

In the garden, whispers rise,
Petals giggle, sharing lies.
"I'm the biggest!" one flower claims,
While daisies play their silly games.

Lilies shout, "Look at my style!"
While sunflowers grin, saying, "Stay awhile!"
Secrets swirl in the balmy air,
Every bud has stories to share.

Roses blush, feeling so grand,
Their thorns ready with a secret plan.
While tulips puff with pride so bright,
In this bloomery, fun is in sight!

So if you wander through their midst,
Join their chatter, don't resist.
For in this garden where the colors beam,
The secrets of joy are more than a dream.

Beneath the Red Veil

Underneath a crimson flair,
Flora chatter, full of air.
They whisper sweet, silly little jokes,
While mischievous vines play pranks on folks.

A banana leaf steals the scene,
Draped like a cape, like a queen!
Petals giggle, hiding their glee,
In this leafy comedy spree.

Leaves rustle, making a fuss,
"Why did the flower cross the bus?"
To blossom out in the fabulous light,
And share its humor, oh what a sight!

So lift the veil, break through the charm,
Join the fun, let nothing harm.
For beneath this bloom's bold smile,
Laughter echoes for endless miles.

Garden of Silent Secrets

In a garden where whispers bloom,
Petals giggle, dispelling gloom.
Plants wear hats, don't ask them why,
They're planning a party, oh me, oh my!

Gnomes dance prancing, shaking their heads,
While ladybugs rest in cozy beds.
Laughter echoes on a soft breeze,
Even the weeds tease the tall trees.

Butterflies flit like playful sprites,
Frogs wear glasses, oh what sights!
A daisy winks, a rose tries to paint,
While the tulips are plotting, oh ain't they quaint!

So wander through this playful space,
Join the fun at nature's pace.
Secrets swirl beneath the sun,
In this garden, laughter's never done!

A Crimson Reverie

A crimson splash with quirky flair,
A flower grins like it just got a dare.
Joking with bees that buzz with delight,
They all laugh together, what a sight!

The petals giggle in the warm sun's rays,
Wiggling around in a merry ballet.
The roots are gossiping, oh what a mess,
A wild rumor about the oak's dress!

In this garden of crimson fun,
Nature's jesters under the sun.
Jokes bloom freely in vibrant hues,
Who knew flowers had such amusing views?

So come take a stroll, let laughter command,
Meet the mischiefs of this floral band.
A rosy smile from each bloom you see,
A light-hearted dance, nature's comedy!

Rich Tones of Nature

In nature's palette, colors play,
With tones so bright they laugh all day.
Leaves wear jackets, adorned with sprinkles,
Nature's humor in rustling crinkles.

The trees converse in whispers bold,
Sharing tales of sun and gold.
A squirrel jokes with a chattering crow,
As flowers shimmy in evening's glow.

Berries blush with laughter's tease,
Swaying softly in the evening breeze.
Each hue a jester, each shade a jest,
In this vibrant world, we find our best.

So roll in the laughter, splash in the scene,
Nature's rich tones are vibrant and keen.
Just listen closely, you may overhear,
The sounds of joy ringing crystal clear!

Emblems of Grace

Emblems frolic in the morning light,
Bowing gently in the soft twilight.
Their petals prance in joyful spins,
While ants wear ties, ready for wins!

The tulips declare, "We're fancy today!"
While daisies giggle in a playful fray.
Graceful moves in the garden air,
With butterflies twirling without a care.

A sunflower smiles with a grand display,
A confident bud in a flowery ballet.
Nature's charm tickles every gaze,
In the wild dance of joyful praise.

So join the waltz of these merry blooms,
For laughter flourishes in nature's rooms.
Each emblem of grace delights the heart,
In this funny farm, we all play a part!

Fluidity of Emotion

In a pot so round and bright,
A plant dances, oh what a sight!
Leaves like arms waving in glee,
Whispering secrets, just wait and see.

Water drips like a funny joke,
The soil chuckles, it's no hoax.
Roots are twirling, having a blast,
Who knew plants could throw such a cast?

Sunshine's laughter, pouring down,
Photosynthesis wears a crown.
With every petal, a vibrant jest,
Plant life's humor, truly the best.

Oh note the bloom, it's grand and absurd,
In a world where silliness is preferred.
Dress it up, make it dance,
In the garden's comedic romance.

Tapestry of Botanical Tales

In the midst of greens and sprays,
Plants gossip in their playful ways.
Cacti crack jokes from the side,
While the daisies giggle and glide.

Leaves weave stories, both short and tall,
Sunflowers hold court, they rule it all.
And violets whisper with a grin,
Who knew being green could be such a win?

The orchids prance, with flair so bold,
Sharing tales of the sun's warm gold.
Pollen parties, oh what fun,
Underneath the bright, happy sun.

Oh, a botanical scene, so quirky and bright,
In this tapestry, joy takes flight.
Every bloom holds a joke, a laugh,
In this garden, we all do the math.

Radiant Sanctuary

In a cozy corner, a plant sits so sweet,
Sipping on sunlight, what a treat!
Its leaves wave, like a friendly hello,
In this radiant space, good vibes flow.

The petals pop with colors galore,
Every bloom knocks on the humor door.
"Don't take life too seriously," cries the fern,
"Join our party, there's much to learn!"

Succulents wink from their sunny perch,
Mimicking laughter, they start to lurch.
Every drop of water's a tickling tease,
In our sanctuary, we all aim to please.

Here's to the blooms that bring us glee,
In this radiant haven, we roam free.
So let's plant a joke, grow a pun,
In this garden, our laughter's never done.

Blooms Beneath the Canopy

Beneath big leaves, where the shadows dance,
Flora gathers for a cheerful prance.
Quiet whispers become playful shouts,
In this jungle vibe, laughter sprouts.

Poppies pop up with a snicker and cheer,
While ferns giggle—can you hear?
Roots play tag, beneath the ground,
Tickling the earth, whispers abound.

The canopy sways, in sync with the fun,
As blossoms debate who's the number one.
"Don't leaf me hanging!" the tulips pout,
As laughter surrounds them all throughout.

In this dance of petals, wild and free,
Every bloom a performer, can't you see?
Comedy blooms where the light filters down,
In this leafy circus, there's no frown.

Blooming Affection

In a garden where plants chat,
One flirts and one falls flat.
The flowers giggle in their beds,
While bees wear tiny flower heads.

A cactus claims to hold a grudge,
While daisies dance, oh, what a fudge!
With greens that shake, they wave in cheer,
Nature's antics wrapped in a sphere.

Petals tease with vibrant hues,
A secret code, see who's the muse!
They gather round for jest and games,
In the sunlight, with no real claims.

So come and join this silly spree,
Where laughter grows on every spree!
Blooming affection in full bloom,
A riot of colors, nothing's doomed!

Nature's Silent Symphony

In the woods, leaves make a laugh,
A squirrel drops his acorn half.
The wind whistles, a curious tune,
As flowers twirl beneath the moon.

Tall trees sway, trying to groove,
While bushes shimmy, in the move.
The sun grins wide, a golden beam,
Nature's orchestra, a funny dream.

Frogs croak out rhythm, oh so bold,
While ants march in, a sight to behold.
Every rustle sounds like humor,
As blossoms burst, the vivid rumor.

With petals swaying; it's quite a sight,
Nature's joke under soft twilight.
In silent symphony, laughter rings,
A chorus of life, oh, how it sings!

Red Echoes in Green

In a patch where colors collide,
Red pops out, it cannot hide.
With cheeky leaves that pull a prank,
The petals dance, a cheeky flank.

A parrot squawks with glee and flair,
While roses blush and curl their hair.
The sun beams down, a playful poke,
While ladybugs play hide and cloak.

Vines entwine for a tickle fight,
Spreading laughter from morn till night.
With blooms that gossip all day long,
In the garden where all belong.

Red echoes ring through vivid scenes,
In leaf and laughter, joy convenes.
Nature's joke has no real bounds,
In the heart where humor resounds!

Dreamscape of Flora

In a dreamscape where petals twirl,
Tulips in hats make quite a whirl.
Lilies flash their frilly skirts,
While daisies gossip, stirring up dirt.

Butterflies play peekaboo,
As violets blush from morning dew.
The sun, a prankster, hides and seeks,
Tickling flowers with sunlight squeaks.

Cacti laugh, "We got the spine!
But watch the thorns, they're divine!"
Each bloom with character, bold and brave,
In this flora dream, we all misbehave.

So come and dance in petals' glow,
Where flowers frolic, putting on a show.
In this landscape of glee, take a chance,
Join the fun in nature's dance!

An Embrace of Flora and Soul

In a garden full of green,
Plants sway like a dancing queen.
One curious bloom starts to grin,
Whispers of happiness within.

Leaves tickle like a playful breeze,
Spreading laughter among the trees.
Petals chat like gossiping pals,
Echoing joy with giggles and lolls.

Roots entwine with a cheeky tease,
Sharing secrets with the buzzing bees.
In this patch of floral delight,
Fun blooms brightly, a cheerful sight.

So let's all join this joyful spree,
Bringing together you and me!
In nature's laughter, we shall bask,
No more questions, just let's ask!

The Lilt of Lush Affection

Dancing around like marionettes,
Flora poses without regrets.
Petals strut with a twinkle in eye,
Who knew plants could fiercely fly?

A dandelion blew its fluffy fluff,
Challenging blooms in a playful puff.
Each sway a flirt, each twist a tease,
Nature's laughter floats on the breeze.

Vines entwined like a romping pair,
Their tangled mess shows they don't care.
Giggling flowers in a vivid show,
Competing for crowns in the garden below.

Bowing low to a tulip's laugh,
Even cactus feels a bit daft.
It's a party under bright sun's blink,
Where every leaf has a chance to wink!

Threads of Vitality Woven

Threads of green in a party cheer,
Petals bounce as they draw near.
With every sway, they giggle bright,
This fabric of life is pure delight.

Every bloom tells a humorous tale,
Of mishaps faced without fail.
One daisy tripped on a sunset's glow,
Wearing laughter like a pro!

Rooted in joy, they conspire,
To make the world bloom with desire.
What a riot in leaves and stems,
Woven threads whisper, 'Be friends!'

So join the fun, don't hold back,
Skip down the path; feel no lack.
In this tapestry of colors and jest,
Flora finds joy, and you'll feel blessed!

In Bloom: A Tale Untold

In a garden where giggles grow,
Each bloom wears a radiant glow.
A sunflower winks, trying to sneak,
While a shy lilac pretends to peek.

Petals play hide and seek with the sun,
Chasing shadows is so much fun!
Each vine twists like a winding road,
Shaping a map of laughter bestowed.

A naughty sprout tickles a bee,
Buzzing back with mischievous glee.
Together they dance in swirling air,
Joyful chaos everywhere!

So come, dear friend, and lend your ear,
To the stories that blooms hold dear.
For in each petal and leaf on the run,
Lies a tale of laughter that's never done!

Enchantment of the Red Crown

In a garden where whispers play,
A flower wore a crown so gay.
It danced with bees, a silly sight,
Swaying to tunes of day and night.

With petals like a jester's cap,
It made the tulips laugh and clap.
'Oh look at me!' it seemed to boast,
While butterflies all cheered and toast.

The sun peeked in, a cheeky grin,
And shadows joined the foolish spin.
Its colors flashed, a shocking scheme,
A vibrant burst, a painter's dream.

The only frown was from a weed,
It sighed, 'I'll never take the lead!'
But in this bloom so bright and bold,
There's joy enough to break the mold.

Echoes of the Jungle

In the jungle, laughter rings,
Where vines can dance and the parrot sings.
A flower blushed with rosy flair,
Mocking its neighbors with squeaks from air.

The monkeys stared with open jaws,
At petals bending just because.
It threw confetti when rain would fall,
Like a party in the jungle hall.

With every breeze, it rocked and swayed,
A glamour queen who never frayed.
'Look at my moves!' it seemed to bray,
As all the critters joined the play.

What a riot, this blooming spree,
Where even ferns would dance with glee!
With colors bright, it drew the crowd,
In nature's show, it felt so proud.

Soft Shadows and Bright Hues

In corners where the sunlight dips,
A flower giggles, rolling its lips.
Amongst the greens, it takes a stand,
A cheeky star in this wild band.

The shadows linger, trying to blend,
But this petal jokes, 'I'll never bend!'
With colors bold, it starts to tease,
'You wish you had my flair with ease!'

Light drips down like honeyed gold,
And every glance, a story told.
With whispering leaves, it sways in tune,
This playful sprite beneath the moon.

While crickets chirp a nightly jest,
It hosts the bravest flower fest.
In soft shadows where laughter flows,
A bit of fun where nobody knows.

Vibrancy of Life's Canvas

On nature's canvas, splashes bright,
A flower posed, a glorious sight.
As bees approached, it winked with glee,
'Oh buzz and sting, come dance with me!'

With strokes of red, it caught the eye,
While nearby tulips sighed a cry.
'Why do they giggle? What's their game?'
'To be so bold, one mustn't be tame!'

Each petal's curve, a grand delight,
Moving to rhythms, pure twilight.
The ants would march in funny lines,
Chasing around on flower vines.

In vibrant hues, the scene was set,
No rules to this painter's duet.
With laughter fresh as springtime air,
Life's canvas blooms without a care.

An Invitation to Growth

Come join us for a dance, oh friend,
With leaves that shimmer, twist, and bend.
Each petal's wink a secret taught,
In this garden, laughter's sought.

Grow tall and proud, don't be shy,
Wave your fronds to the bright blue sky.
Let's sprout some jokes, let's stretch and sway,
In this leafy hall, we'll play all day.

So plant your feet and wiggle your roots,
Let's share wild dreams in our fancy boots.
With every giggle, stretch, and spin,
Our leafy fun will surely begin!

So grab a friend and just let go,
In this vibrant grove, the joy will grow.
With every petal, let laughter bloom,
In this sunny spot, there's always room!

The Essence of Blooming

In sunny spots where we gather bright,
A quirky plant will steal the light.
With petals swirling, colors bold,
Each tale it whispers is pure gold.

Prancing petals, they sway and twirl,
A daily dose of leafy swirl.
With every chuckle shared in bloom,
We chase away the afternoon gloom.

Laughter spills like raindrops sweet,
As roots and friends all twine and meet.
In this party of blooms, take a seat,
Where dancing leaves are quite the treat!

So shine on bright, you funny flower,
Spread joy and giggles with every hour.
In this garden, we find our way,
Let's bloom together, hip-hip-hooray!

Crimson Passions

In a world of crimson, bold and bright,
A cheeky flower sets its sights.
With winky blooms and sassy flair,
It struts around without a care.

Passion's red, and it knows the score,
Making friends at every door.
With every giggle, petals clap,
In this loving garden, we'll overlap.

Cuddly leaves whisper soft and sweet,
Sharing secrets with every beat.
A blushing bloom, a heart so fine,
Entwined in laughter, yours and mine.

So bring your spark and let it shine,
In this wacky grove, everything's fine!
With petals laughing, come take a chance,
In the crimson light, let's dance, dance, dance!

A Shelter of Leaves

Underneath the canopy wide,
A giggling plant is our guide.
With rustling leaves that sway and tease,
Building laughter among the trees.

Here in the shade where fun takes flight,
We share our stories 'til it's night.
With twinkling eyes and playful roots,
Gather 'round in our leafy shoots.

Each branch a friend where jokes arise,
In this shelter, no need for disguise.
With every breeze, our spirits lift,
In this laughter grove, we find our gift.

So come on over, don't be shy!
Find your joy, and let it fly.
Among the greens and chuckles sweet,
This leafy haven can't be beat!

Passionate Breezes

In the garden, where plants chat,
A whispering breeze sings to the cat.
The flowers giggle, swaying up high,
While bees do a dance, oh me, oh my!

Leaves tumble down with a flouncy flair,
A beetle declares, 'I'm the best in here!'
They argue and bicker like pros on stage,
Nature's own sitcom, turning a page.

A squirrel joins in, with a quirky frown,
As petals start twirling, losing their crown.
With laughter and joy, the scene unfolds,
In this vibrant party, all life beholds.

So here's to the blooms, so bold and bright,
Their colorful antics, a sheer delight!
In this floral realm, all worries cease,
Every tiny laugh brings us sweet peace.

A Scarlet Story

A bold little plant, in a pot so red,
Holds secret tales that swirl in its head.
With petals like laughter, it winks at the sun,
'Look folks, I'm fabulous, and oh so fun!'

A bumblebee jokes, buzzing here and there,
'Is it hot in here or is it just your flair?'
Each drop of dew, a story to tell,
A comedy show only nature can sell.

The blooms exchange whispers, a gossiping spree,
'Did you see the squirrel? Thought he was a bee!'
They chuckle together, all in good jest,
In this scarlet saga, they wear their best vest.

So join in the laughter, let colors inspire,
As petals share secrets wrapped in desire.
In the lushest of realms, joy finds a way,
With every bright blossom, we play all day!

Threads of Nature's Fabric

In a world sewn together, patchworks delight,
Yarns of green laughter, a colorful sight.
The flowers debate on the best shade of hue,
'I'm the star of the garden!' 'No, it's all you!'

A rogue dandelion swings by with grace,
Fluffing up petals, just to pick up the pace.
'Don't thread it too tight, or we'll lose our fun,'
As bees craft their tunes, work never is done.

Textures of nature, with quirks to unfold,
In this playful tapestry, stories retold.
A mix of the wild, a splash of the tame,
Each stitch in this fabric adds to the game.

So come take a look, at the silliness spun,
In this woven world, oh how we all run!
Through blossoms and laughter, life's fabric we weave,
Frolicking joyfully, in what we believe!

Shelter of Delicate Petals

Under petals so cozy, we find our laughs,
A resting place where mischief crafts.
Tiny critters giggle, with a splash of cheer,
'Who brought the sunbeams? They're far too dear!'

A ladybug prances, with dots of red glee,
In this snug little nook, so happy and free.
The petals conspire, with each gentle sway,
'Let's tuck in the sunlight; we can play all day!'

When raindrops tap lightly, they start a spree,
Creating a shower, a fresh comedy.
With splashes of mirth, the flowers take flight,
In their snug canopy, we dance through the night.

So gather 'round blooms, let's enjoy the show,
In this petal-wrapped haven, let laughter flow.
A shelter of stories, where friendship grows strong,
In the arms of good humor, we all belong!

Whispers of the Earth

In the garden where flowers play,
Talk about dirt in a funny way.
Plants gossip like they're in a chat,
"Did you hear? The rose is a brat!"

Bees buzz loudly, they laugh and hum,
"Sneaky snails think they're still so yum!"
While daisies shake in a breezy dance,
Giving lilies a flirty glance.

Roots tickle in the soil below,
"Who knew that carrots could be so slow?"
Every leaf has a story to tell,
In this silly leafy citadel!

The sun winks over each vibrant hue,
Plants are comedians, who knew?
Nature's a stage with no end in sight,
Where every blossom is ready to write!

Colors of Unspoken Love

Petals blush as they flirt with the breeze,
Whispers of romance hide amongst the leaves.
What's a flower to do with a crush?
Just sway and shimmer, in the evening hush.

A sunflower stalks, so tall and proud,
Winks at a daisy wrapped in a cloud.
"Hey, pretty petal, mind if I swing?"
But the daisy giggles, 'That's not my thing!'

Tulips blush red like they've seen a dream,
But violets chuckle, causing a scene.
"With love so bright, don't cover your face,
Just be yourself, and own your space!"

In this garden of secrets, laughter's the art,
Where colors unite, and joy's off the chart.
Every bloom has a tale, no need to hide,
In the rhythm of blooms, love's the guide!

Within the Crimson Core

In the center of petals, secrets fold tight,
A red little riddle, hiding from sight.
"What do you think? I'm not a cherry!"
Says the shy bud, feeling quite merry.

Caterpillars joke as they munch and chew,
"This salad bar? Just for me and you!"
While ladybugs giggle, playing their game,
Smeared with spots, it's a colorful fame.

With a whispering breeze, petals twist and twirl,
Jokes of the garden, as the flowers curl.
"Do you know the one about bees and their flight?"
"They always party, from morning till night!"

So dive into color, where laughter ignites,
In the blooms of the day and the whispers of nights.
Every red blush and petal-shaped grin,
Unlocks the joy that's hidden within!

The Allure of Flora

Oh, how the blossoms giggle so bright,
Dressed in colors, what a delightful sight!
"Flora, dear friend, you're quite the tease,
But have you heard the earthworms' sneeze?"

Cacti boast their spikes, trying to impress,
While tulips blow kisses, in playful excess.
"Got no thorns, but I'm oh so chic!"
As pansies laugh, saying, "Oh, you're weak!"

A clumsy bee buzzes, tripping on dew,
Stumbling through petals, like a clumsy crew.
"I came for the nectar, but stayed for the fun,
What a party of scents, I'm not yet done!"

Every spray of fragrance tells a joke anew,
The plants all giggle, that's just what they do.
In the allure of flora, laughter takes flight,
Where fun blooms eternal, and every day's bright!

The Language of Unfurling Leaves

In the garden of whispers and sighs,
Leaves giggle as they reach for the skies.
With every curl, they craft a new tale,
Of sunlit dances and love's grand trail.

Petals would gossip, if only they could,
In the chatter of pollen, they'd speak for good.
Their colors would clash, like a bickering crew,
Yet somehow, they shine in their chaotic view.

Stems roll their eyes at the leaves' playful tease,
'Oh, to be young again!' they whisper with ease.
While roots snicker lowly from their earthy bed,
"Don't take it too seriously! Just enjoy the spread!"

So next time you wander in floral delight,
Remember the laughter that fills up the night.
For nature's bouquet is a laugh riot too,
In the language of leaves, there's always a clue.

Embers of Botanical Romance

In a pot of romance, the flirtatious vines,
Twirl like new lovers, sipping on wines.
Leaves whisper secrets under the moon,
While dormant buds wake to a springtime tune.

A cactus feels lonely, with spikes all around,
Searching for love in this prickly ground.
But roses, so bold, just laugh at the joke,
Sharing their petals with every fine bloke.

A daisy declared, 'I'm the one you adore!'
But the carnation chimed in, "I've got much more!"
Together they giggled, the petals align,
In the world of lush greens, it's all love divine.

When blossoms collide, it's a whimsical sight,
With laughter and color igniting the night.
In this garden of giggles and fragrant romps,
Every petal's a burst, and love often stomps.

An Infinite Blooming

In a garden so vast, where silliness grows,
Every flower insists it knows how to pose.
With beaming bright colors, they outshine the sun,
As they wink at the bees, just having some fun.

A tulip once claimed, "I'm the best in the field!"
But a dandelion laughed, "Oh, do you yield?"
For in every wild bloom, there's a story to tell,
Of roots and of shoots, where we all dwell well.

When petals begin to trade tips on finesse,
The orchids are known for their floral excess.
"I'm fancy," they smirk, while the daisies roll eyes,
In this harmonious brawl, no one truly complies.

So dance with the blooms, let your laughter take flight,
In gardens that bloom with sheer joy, pure delight.
For in every soft petal is a giggle's refrain,
In an infinite blooming, we all share the gain.

Radiance in Every Vein

In the bright, sunny patch where the laughter is seen,
Each leaf whispers joy, bright and evergreen.
With veins like a roadmap to giggle and grin,
They flaunt their bright wisdom, inviting all in.

"Oh look at me," cries the proud little leaf,
"I'm the spoonful of joy in this botanical chief!"
Glancing at neighbors that sway with delight,
In this leafy parade, everyone's bright.

When shadows cast doubt on the leaves' vibrant show,
They tickle the branches, watch laughter grow.
With sunlight as fuel, they sparkle and beam,
Emitting sweet warmth, like a botanical dream.

So join in the fun of this colorful spree,
In gardens of giggles, you're welcome, you see!
For with every vein shimmering brightly in green,
There's humor and joy that can always be gleaned.

The Allure of Crimson Curves

In a pot, she sways with glee,
Her petals shine, oh so free.
Bold and bright, a floral tease,
Dancing lightly in the breeze.

With a wink, she catches the eye,
Sipping sunlight, oh my, oh my!
In a dress of red, she's got style,
Making neighbors grin all the while.

Her leaves whisper gossip so sweet,
While insects gather round for a treat.
"Come closer, boys, don't be shy!"
She coos with a rustle and sigh.

Yet when the weather turns drear,
She needs love, and that's crystal clear.
A little water, and she's fine,
Sprouting smiles with every vine.

In the Shade of Leafy Emotions

Under the canopy, gossip flows,
With leaves swirling in playful rows.
Tales of love shared on a stem,
A banquet of sunshine, come join the gem!

Petals blush with laughter bright,
As the ants party through the night.
In emerald arms, they're dancing too,
The scent of mischief wafts right through.

"Catch me if you can!" she says with flair,
Though none can match her vibrant air.
Frogs croak a melody on repeat,
As the blooms sway to their own beat.

In this jungle of love and zeal,
Every curve helps us to feel.
With humor wrapped in every leaf,
Life's a joyful, floral motif.

Where Love Meets the Tropics

A sunny spot amidst coconuts,
She giggles while mocking the mutes.
Her bloom's a promise, sweet and bold,
Whispering secrets, never old.

In the tropics where laughter's found,
She spins tales with a twist profound.
"Hey there, bees, don't spread too wide,
You might trip on leaves when you glide!"

With jungle beats, she dances along,
Her colors pop, like a vibrant song.
"Watch my moves, I'm quite the sight,
Join my fiesta, dance through the night!"

Where love blooms with such daring flair,
A garden party whispers through the air.
In every petal, a story's spun,
A riot of joy, oh what fun!

Nature's Crimson Whisper

In the garden, secrets play,
A red temptation brightens the day.
With cheeky blooms that nod and sway,
She giggles at the sun's warm ray.

"Come cuddle closer," she seems to sing,
As butterflies flutter, doing their thing.
Crimson curves in dazzling display,
Helping hearts find their way.

When raindrops fall, they tap her head,
She pouts like a queen in her floral bed.
Yet laughter sparkles through the gloom,
Even in chaos, she seeks to bloom.

So here's to blooms with a fun-filled tease,
Whispering promises with such ease.
In every garden, let joy unfurl,
Sprinkle laughter in this floral whirl.

Inflorescence of Untold Stories

In a garden filled with chatter,
The blooms tell tales of laughter.
With petals dressed in vibrant clothes,
They gossip sweetly, who then knows?

The bees are buzzin' with delight,
As flowers dance in morning light.
They break the rules of floral flair,
And twirl like they just don't care.

A sprinkle here, a pollen there,
These blooms suggest a wild affair.
They prance and sway from stalk to stalk,
While squirrels tease with playful talk.

Underneath the sun, they play,
A chorus bright, they laugh all day.
With all their fun, you'd think it's grand,
A colorful world, a merry band.

A Sanctuary in Color

In gardens bright and full of cheer,
The petals whisper, "Come right here!"
With colors wild and shapes that twist,
You'd think they practiced for a list.

The daisies wink, the roses blush,
While violets giggle in a hush.
Each bloom has secrets tucked away,
They plot adventures in the clay.

In shadows deep, the ferns do sway,
While daisies joke and frolic play.
They share their dreams with every breeze,
And mold their hopes among the leaves.

A canvas bright, so fun and free,
A sanctuary, come laugh with me!
With every hue, there's glee to find,
These flowers leave no souls behind.

Nature's Heartbeat Within

Amidst the greens, the blossoms thrive,
In colors bright, they feel alive.
They jest and jive as breezes blow,
With rhythm that we all can know.

A jesting bud, a cheeky bloom,
They giggle softly, fill the room.
With puns of photosynthesis,
They share their cleverness, oh yes!

The petals strut, a lively crew,
In shades of pink, orange, and blue.
They frolic on the gentle breeze,
Inviting all to join with ease.

In their embrace, the world feels light,
With every laugh, a pure delight.
Nature's rhythm beats so bold,
In each bright petal, stories told.

The Serenade of Sunlit Blooms

When daylight sings, the blooms arise,
They giggle under sunny skies.
With every twirl, they catch a ray,
And flirt with clouds throughout the day.

The sunbeams tickle, petals blush,
As blooms enjoy a morning hush.
Each flower shares a silly plot,
While gathering friends with every shot.

In the spotlight, they love to pose,
Fashionistas in garden clothes.
With every sway, a grand ballet,
They waltz and chatter, come what may.

So join the fun, don't be shy,
In this affair, the blooms comply.
A serenade of colors bright,
A garden full of pure delight.

Ties that Bind in Botanicals

In a garden of oddities, we do play,
Each leaf a jester on display.
With colors like pizza, and shapes of a shoe,
Nature's own circus, we laugh through and through.

Among blooms in a riddle that twist and twine,
The petals giggle, sharing a vine.
Who knew a plant could wear such a grin?
In this leafy a comedy, we all fit right in.

So next time you're lost in the green of it all,
Remember the plants have a ball at the mall.
If you hear them chuckle or see them sway,
Just know that they're having a fun, silly day!

From fronds that dance to blooms that chat,
Each one a character, imagine that!
The ties that bind in this botanical spree,
Bring joy to the heart, and a chuckle to me.

A Red Symphony in Stillness.

A swirl of crimson where stillness sings,
With petals like capes and roots like springs.
They whisper of secrets in the hush of the night,
In this silent concert, everything's bright.

A laugh from the branches, a wink from the leaf,
It's a comedy show, though it looks like grief.
The flowers play chess while the sprouts dance around,
In this cozy theater, joy's always found.

When threats come calling, they bloom and they bend,
Like actors pretending, on each other they depend.
A rhapsody of red in every small petal,
Leaves giggle together, a green confetti medal.

So sink into stillness, let laughter abide,
For this vibrant symphony swings wide,
In a world where colors and giggles entwine,
Each petal a solo, in humor divine!

Crimson Whisper

In the garden of giggles, a soft voice does call,
A crimson whisper, like a prank on us all.
Petals that linger and play hide-and-seek,
Catch me if you can—oh, the joy is unique!

The leaves gossip softly, sharing a joke,
As bees buzz along, like a ticklish poke.
With each little rustle, a chuckle does brew,
I swear those blossoms are laughing at you!

In shadows and sunlight, they tease and they twirl,
Like dancers in bloom, making the world whirl.
With roots that are silly and stems that are spry,
This riot of crimson makes spirits fly high!

So next time you wander through petals so fine,
Listen close to whispers, and you'll surely find,
Nature's own humor in this magical place,
A crimson world where laughter's embraced!

Nectar of Resilience

In the midst of a storm, they stand up and grin,
With roots like superheroes, they just won't give in.
Sipping rain like nectar, they're ready to laugh,
Through trials and troubles, not a hint of a gaffe.

Their petals are tough, yet so sweet to the taste,
With sunlight for breakfast, there's no time to waste.
They dance in the wind, with roots deeply set,
Each drop of resilience, they've got it, you bet!

In this garden of joy, there's no space for dread,
Not a single petal's ever seen feeling dead.
Each flower a story, a punchline, a cheer,
In the face of the odds, they persevere here!

So raise up your glass to these blooms strong and bright,
With nectar of laughter that sparkles with light.
In the comedy of life, with grit and some flair,
These plants show us all how to grow in the air!

Geometry of Delicate Leaves

In the garden, a leaf did prance,
With angles sharp, it took a chance.
It wiggled and jived in the sun's embrace,
Drawing shapes with a quirky grace.

Nearby, a flower tried to sway,
Said, "I can dance, come join the soiree!"
But the leaf just laughed, its form so neat,
"I'm all about angles, you can't compete!"

A bee buzzed by with a cheeky grin,
"You both look silly, let's join in!"
So they spun around, in a floral rave,
Geometry's fun when you misbehave!

Sunlight's laughter glanced off the green,
As leaves and blooms danced, a whimsical scene.
So remember, dear friend, in the garden's reprieve,
Even shapes can join in and make us believe!

Tides of Serenity

In the pond, I saw a frog,
Bouncing about like a quirky dog.
It croaked a tune that made me smile,
Wading through water, with perfect style.

The lily pads swayed in rhythmic glee,
"I'm the captain!" the frog yelled, "Follow me!"
They drifted along, a floating parade,
While fish beneath giggled, unafraid.

Suddenly a duck made a splashy dive,
"Am I late for the party?"   it seemed alive!
The frog just chuckled, reining his crew,
"Join our flotilla, there's snacks for you!"

Even the sun wore goofy rays,
As all joined in the water's ballet.
In the tides of joy, let troubles cease,
For nature's laughter brings us peace.

Love's Gentle Reflection

In the mirror, I saw a grin,
A wiggle, a dance, oh what a spin!
With twinkling eyes, I made a face,
"Reflections of love should be full of grace!"

But the mirror chuckled, gave me a wink,
"You dance like a leaf, just take a drink!"
So I twirled and slipped, made quite the mess,
In love's mirror, I felt more than blessed.

A heart-shaped balloon bounced in the air,
"Float here with me, if you dare!"
We giggled together, floating so free,
Reflecting joy, just you and me!

In that moment, all troubles behind,
Love's silly game, the heart's own find.
Laughter echoed in every glance,
For love is best when you take a chance!

Colors of Longing

In a box of crayons, colors sought,
Each one a dream, in knots they fought.
Red wanted blue, to dance in the sky,
While yellow dreamed of the sun's sly eye.

"Let's paint the world!" said green with cheer,
"We'll splash about, nothing to fear!"
But purple sighed, a hue so bright,
"Without a partner, I can't take flight!"

The colors giggled, a riotous spree,
"Let's mix together, just wait and see!"
So they swirled in dreams, a vibrant mess,
Longing for a canvas, oh what a quest!

Across the page, a rainbow did bloom,
With laughter in strokes, they filled the room.
Colors rejoiced, in friendship's embrace,
For the joy of longing brought smiles to the space.

Tender Caress of Rain

Tiny droplets dance and play,
Tickling leaves on a sunny day.
They giggle as they take a leap,
Splashing joy, their secrets keep.

A drizzle looks like nature's jest,
As flowers wear their raindrop vest.
With every splash, they seem to grin,
The garden's laughter, a joyful spin.

Puddles form like little ponds,
Where ants perform their silly swans.
Each leaf adorned, a nature's crown,
They peek at life, never a frown.

So here we stand, umbrellas tossed,
In sprightly rain, we're never lost.
With every drop, life's fun unfolds,
A drippy tale that never grows old.

Breath of a Blossom

A petal smiles with morning's grace,
In a sunbeam's warm embrace.
It whispers softly, 'Come and see!'
As bees buzz by, and ants agree.

With every breath, it tells a joke,
A breeze tickles, the laughter's woke.
The colors clash in playful cheer,
Painting petals, far and near.

'Excuse me, friend, you're in my way!'
Chirps a bud, with sass at play.
They twirl and twist with vibrant flair,
A floral dance in fragrant air.

So stop and smell, but don't forget,
The fun that blooms is never set.
For in each bloom a tale is spun,
In this mad garden, we have fun!

An Invitation to Wonder

Step into the garden, take a peek,
Where daisies gossip, and blossoms speak.
When violets wink and poppies sway,
The flowers invite you to come and play.

They giggle and jive in vibrant hues,
Sharing their tales of morning dews.
'You think you're tall? Just see us here!'
Stems stretch up high with garden cheer.

A daffodil dons a sunny hat,
While pansies ponder, 'What's up with that?'
In this wild mix of colors and fun,
Every petal shines, a little pun.

So join the laughter, let worries cease,
In this bloom ballet, find your peace.
For nature's giggle is open wide,
An invitation with flowers as guides.

Resilient Flourish

In the face of storms, they sway and bend,
Our leafy friends, nature's joyful trend.
With roots so solid, they take a stand,
Defying the odds, they dance on land.

With every gust, they wave hello,
While chattering leaves put on a show.
'We won't back down!' they seem to say,
As they pirouette in wild ballet.

A daisy tripped, but up it sprang,
With a chuckle, through blooms, it sang.
'It's just a tumble, not a fall!'
These brave little fighters, standing tall.

So here's to growth, and here's to cheer,
With every bloom, we persevere.
In the garden of life, we flourish bright,
With laughter as armor, we spread delight.

Pulse of the Rainforest

In the jungle, green and bright,
A flower dons its red delight.
Bees are buzzing, ants are bold,
This plant's got stories to be told.

With leaves so big, it makes a scene,
A plant that's king, or so it seems.
A leaf could serve as a good brigade,
For all the critters on parade.

It dances in the wind's sweet blow,
Swaying to the rhythms that they know.
A tropical diva takes her stand,
With style and flair that's quite unplanned.

So raise a glass, let laughter spring,
To floral friends who love to sing.
In this wild place, let spirits soar,
A vital pulse in nature's core!

Veins of Passion

In leafy hats adorned with glee,
A floral star that's bold and free.
With ribbed attire, they strut around,
A fashion show that can astound.

Each petal flaunts a cheeky grin,
A leaf that's ready to begin.
With roots that joke, and vines that tease,
This plant makes playtime with such ease.

They sip the sun like it's a drink,
In bright costumes, they never sink.
A playful bunch, they're on the chase,
To sunbathe in this lively space.

Giggles echo in the breeze,
As nature shares her quirks with ease.
This plant, with humor in its game,
Is always up for some flower fame!

Island's Embrace

Splashed in hues of berry bright,
A tropical twist that feels just right.
It waves to time with petals wide,
Each laugh, a bloom, it cannot hide.

On sun-kissed shores where breezes play,
The flowers giggle the day away.
In circles, they do cha-cha cha,
"Join the fun!" they say from afar.

With roots deep down, they hum a tune,
Twisting in laughter 'neath the moon.
An uproar of colors in a row,
This plant's a star, putting on a show!

So come and dance, let spirits mix,
With nature's jesters, we have our fix.
In this embrace, we twirl and spin,
A vibrant life that's sure to win!

Symbols of Eternal Spring

In gardens lush where laughter dwells,
Each petal tells its funny tales.
With comic grace, they stand so tall,
A laughing stock, who'd dare to fall?

They poke their heads up, bold and bright,
"Look at me!" they shout with delight.
With every glance, a chuckle spills,
Their antics bring us such sweet thrills.

In vibrant hues, they jive and jump,
These playful blooms, they laugh and thump.
In every breeze, a joke flies free,
This floral jest is pure jubilee!

So raise your voice and let it sing,
For flowers that bring joy in spring.
In laughter's bloom, we find our fate,
With nature's humor, oh, so great!

Sheltered Sentiments

In a pot of laughter and cheer,
A plant whispers secrets, oh dear!
With leaves all shiny and bright,
It claims it fears the night.

Twirling roots in a playful sway,
Saying, "Keep those bugs away!"
Joking with water, it takes a sip,
"I'm the queen, just check my grip!"

Wishing for sun, or maybe shade,
With each tiny leaf, a grand parade.
It tells the sun, "You're just too hot!"
Twirling around, giving all it's got.

In its green world, it rules the scene,
With every petal, it reigns supreme.
Watch it dance with a playful thrill,
Hiding secrets, yet giving a chill!

A Dance of Red and Desire

A crimson queen on her throne,
Wobbling leaves, making it known.
Watch her shake, oh what a sight,
She pledges to bloom every night!

"Come see my friends, the bees in flight!"
She giggles, twirling with delight.
Her petals sway in a sexy jig,
"Join my party, don't be a twig!"

She twirls in a dress of vibrant hue,
Promises chaos, fun, and a view.
"Who knew a plant would be so sly?"
Gossip she shares, oh my, oh my!

With the breeze, she starts to tease,
"Bring the laughter, I'll bring the breeze!"
In this garden, the revelry grows,
A dance of secrets, as everyone knows!

Secrets of the Bold Blossom

In whispers shared among the greens,
A flower flaunts like it's in scenes.
With cheerful petals shouting, "Look!"
Hearts flutter, capturing the crook.

"Why be plain when you can be loud?"
It chuckles, prouder than a crowd.
"Step closer now, I'll spill the tea,
I'm the best-kept secret, can't you see?"

Talented in charming all the bugs,
With tricks that lavish and tug at hugs.
"It's a blooming deal, just wait and see,
Once you're here, you'll never be free!"

It blooms and giggles, stretching wide,
Like a comedian, never can hide.
Watch it twinkle, with a wink—a gift,
In this flower's realm, hearts will lift!

Beneath the Scarlet Veil

Beneath the cloak of dazzling red,
A mischief brews like buttered bread.
Petals whisper, "What's the plan?"
Impromptu dances that began!

"Link arms with me and twirl away,
We'll bloom together, come what may!"
It winks at friends in the garden,
A floral bash, oh, who's the hardest?

With each gust of wind, a giggle escapes,
From sunny smiles to breeze-shaped capes.
"Do you see the ants, they just can't dance?
Poor little guys, they've no romance!"

So gather 'round, let spirits rise,
Under this veil, no need for guise.
In whispered joy, adventure calls,
With little blooms, we'll share it all!